THE 7-STEP FORMULA FOR LAUNCHING A SIX-FIGURE ONLINE BUSINESS

Ignite Your Online Business Dreams: The Ultimate Guide to a Six-Figure Digital Venture"

JONAS CHARLES KPABITEY

Copyright © 2024 JONAS CHARLES KPABITEY

All rights reserved.
No part of this publication may be reproduced, distributed, or transmitted in any form or by any means, including photocopying, recording, or other electronic or mechanical methods, without the prior written permission of the copyright owner, except in the case of brief quotations embodied in critical reviews and certain other noncommercial uses permitted by copyright law. For permission requests, please contact]
Phone number +233 (0) 555848312
+233 (0) 506692718
Email address:
CharlesWashington783@gmail.com

"In the digital realm, success is crafted with precision, not chance. Master the seven steps to unleash the power of your online ambition and pave the path to six-figure triumph."

CONTENTS

Title Page
Copyright
Epigraph
Foreword
Introduction
Preface
Chapter 1   1
Chapter 2   4
Chapter 3   7
Chapter 4:   12
Chapter 5:   17
Chapter 6:   21
Chapter 7:   28
Epilogue   33
Afterword   35
About The Author   37

FOREWORD

This is "The 7-Step Formula for Launching a Six-Figure Online Business." In the fast-paced world of entrepreneurship, the digital environment provides unique chances for those who are ready to take them. Whether you're an experienced company owner trying to develop your internet presence or a first-time entrepreneur, this book is your road map to success.

Drawing on years of expertise in the online business world, the author has simplified the critical stages required to establish a flourishing online company. From establishing your specialty and creating your brand to mastering marketing methods and developing your company, each chapter offers concrete insights and practical tips to help you reach six-figure status.

As you begin on this road, keep in mind that creating a successful internet company involves effort, tenacity, and the ability to adapt to change. To remain ahead of the competition, embrace difficulties, learn from your experiences, and harness the force of innovation.

Whether you want to be financially independent, relocate, or just pursue your passion, "The 7-Step Formula for Launching a Six-Figure Online Business" can help you make your dreams a reality. So get in, take notes, and prepare for a transforming path to online business success.

Best wishes for your business aspirations.

INTRODUCTION

An era of never-before-seen entrepreneurial possibility has been brought about by the digital revolution. There has never been more opportunity for prospective business owners to create flourishing, profitable ventures as the globe shifts more and more towards the ease and accessibility of internet shopping. But there are obstacles in the way of starting a successful online business. The process can seem overwhelming, especially for those who are just getting started, from creating an effective business plan and developing a strong online presence to negotiating the difficulties of running an online store and obtaining the required capital.

This book fills that need. The all-inclusive guide "The 7-Step Formula for Launching a Six-Figure Online Business" can help you turn your entrepreneurial aspirations into a profitable reality. You will find in these pages a methodical and tested technique for creating a profitable online business, one that I have personally used to establish and hone through my own experiences as a six-figure online business owner.

This book has a transforming 7-step technique that has the capacity to rekindle your business spirit and unleash your full potential. Whether you're a seasoned professional looking to make the switch to digital or a first-time entrepreneur with fresh ideas, this formula will provide you with the knowledge, strategies, and actionable steps you need to navigate the ever-changing landscape of online business.

On this voyage, you will:
1. Investigate the attractiveness and promise of internet entrepreneurship and determine your unique value proposition.
2. Create a solid and adaptive business strategy to lay the

groundwork for your internet venture. 3. Create an appealing online presence, which includes a user-friendly website and a powerful brand image.

4. Understand the fundamentals of e-commerce, from product management and payment processing to logistics and fulfilment.

5. Secure the funds required to realise your online company ideas.

6. Use scalable growth strategies and success concepts to build your online empire.

7. Ensure long-term viability by improving operations, managing funds, and overcoming legal issues.

By the time you finish reading this book, you will have gained the knowledge and self-assurance necessary to start a lucrative six-figure internet business, as well as a profound comprehension of the entrepreneurial mindset and the fortitude required to overcome any obstacles that may arise. Are you prepared to start this life-changing adventure? Let's get started and discover the keys to creating a successful internet business of your own.

PREFACE

The year was 2020, and the globe was dealing with an unparalleled global crisis. A paradigm change was taking place amidst the uncertainty and turbulence, altering the landscape of entrepreneurship for the rest of time. As businesses of all sizes dealt with the pandemic's obstacles, a new generation of internet entrepreneurs developed, grasping the opportunity afforded by the digital frontier.

I was among them. Like many others, I had long wanted to start my own online business, but the moment had never been right. That is, until the events of 2020 compelled me to reconsider my objectives and take a chance. With nothing to lose and everything to gain, I set out on a mission to turn my entrepreneurial dreams into a thriving reality. It wasn't an easy route. Initially, I faced numerous challenges, ranging from developing an engaging web presence and navigating the complexity of e-commerce to securing the necessary capital and taking my firm to new heights. But I remained strong, propelled by an unyielding trust in the potential of cyberspace.

It did indeed change mine. Today, I am the happy owner of a six-figure online business that has not only provided me with financial independence and personal fulfilment, but has also enabled me to inspire and motivate others to embark on their own entrepreneurial paths. This experience - the victories and tribulations, the lessons learned and insights acquired - is what I have written about in these pages. "The 7-Step Formula for Launching a Six-Figure Online Business" is a detailed road map that will walk aspiring entrepreneurs like you through the transformative process of turning your ambitions into a successful reality.

These chapters will teach you the critical methods, tactics, and attitude modifications required to negotiate the evolving world of internet entrepreneurship. From developing a winning business strategy and establishing a strong online presence to mastering the art of e-commerce and taking your company to new heights, this book will provide you with the tools and information you need to overcome barriers and reach your full potential. Whether you're a seasoned professional wishing to transfer into the digital sphere, or a first-time entrepreneur with unique ideas, this book is your ultimate companion on the route to developing a successful and profitable online business.

These chapters will teach you the critical methods, tactics, and attitude modifications required to negotiate the evolving world of internet entrepreneurship. From developing a winning business strategy and establishing a strong online presence to mastering the art of e-commerce and taking your company to new heights, this book will provide you with the tools and information you need to overcome barriers and reach your full potential. Whether you're a seasoned professional wishing to transfer into the digital sphere, or a first-time entrepreneur with unique ideas, this book is your ultimate companion on the route to developing a successful and profitable online business.

So let us go on this amazing trip together. The route may not be simple, but I am convinced that with the appropriate mindset, techniques, and support, you, too, can accomplish the success you desire. It's time to reignite your entrepreneurial spirit and turn your online business dreams into a six-figure reality.

CHAPTER 1

Ignite Your Online Business Ambition

Examining the Appeal and Possibilities of Internet Entrepreneurship

An unprecedented period of opportunity for entrepreneurs has been brought about by the digital revolution. The cost of launching a profitable internet business has never been cheaper thanks to the growth of social media, e-commerce platforms, and worldwide connection. The potential for financial independence, location flexibility, and access to a large consumer base are just a few of the reasons why Internet entrepreneurship is so alluring to would-be business owners.

Digital firms' inherent flexibility and scalability are at the heart of their attraction. Unlike traditional brick-and-mortar endeavours, online businesses may be run from anywhere in the world, allowing for previously unthinkable levels of location independence and work-life balance. Furthermore, the data-driven nature of digital commerce gives entrepreneurs important insights and the capacity to make informed, data-driven decisions on everything from understanding customer behaviour to optimising marketing campaigns and measuring the effectiveness of various efforts.

The genuine potential of online entrepreneurship, however, resides in its capacity to overcome geographical constraints. With the correct ideas and execution, an internet business may rapidly develop its customer base and revenue streams at a low incremental cost. Scalability is an important advantage since it allows internet business owners to access a worldwide audience and achieve exceptional growth without being constrained by physical location. It's no surprise, then, that the promise of financial freedom, location independence, and the opportunity to build a scalable, data-driven enterprise has sparked the entrepreneurial spirit of countless people, from seasoned professionals looking for a new challenge to aspiring first-time business owners with innovative ideas. The digital revolution has ushered in a new era of business opportunities, laying the way for online business success story.

Identifying Your Unique Value Proposition and Target Market

The first step in becoming an internet entrepreneur is to determine your unique value proposition and target market. This important process will not only inform the core of your business strategy, but will also direct the development of your products, services, and marketing efforts. Your online business's unique value proposition (UVP) is the specific, tangible benefit it provides to customers. It is what distinguishes you from the competition and persuades your target audience to choose your offering over competitors. A strong UVP is brief, appealing, and effectively addresses your ideal customer's pain points or needs.

Begin by researching your target market thoroughly to identify your unique selling point. Who are the people or businesses who would benefit the most from your products or services? What are their individual requirements, challenges, and preferences? Understanding your target demographic at a granular level will allow you to create a UVP that speaks to them on a deeper level. Next, consider your own skills, expertise, and any unique resources or competencies you bring to the table. How will you use these assets to provide unique value to your target customers? What distinguishes your product or service from the competition?

You may need to test and improve your messaging several times before you discover the ideal balance when creating a compelling value proposition. Keep in mind that your UVP needs to be memorable, succinct, and expressed in a clear and concise manner through all of your sales and marketing channels. Refining your target market is the next step after defining your UVP. Who specifically are the people or companies that your offering is most likely to appeal to? To create an accurate image of your ideal client, take into account elements like online behavior, psychographics, pain areas, and demographics.

By establishing your unique selling point and target market, you will be able to create a laser-focused business strategy, specialised products and services, and marketing messages that resonate with your audience. This foundational work will not only lay the groundwork for a successful online business launch, but it will also equip you with the strategic direction and focus required to navigate the ever-changing environment of internet entrepreneurship.

CHAPTER 2

Laying the Groundwork - Crafting a Winning Business Plan

Conducting Comprehensive Market Research

Thorough market research serves as the foundation for each successful online company effort. You'll be able to make educated decisions, mitigate risks, and position your company for long-term success if you have a thorough awareness of your target market, the competitive environment, and industry trends. The first step in conducting market research is to determine your target audience. **Who are the people and businesses who would benefit the most from your products or services**? Create a complete consumer persona by delving deeply into their demographics, psychographics, internet behaviour, and pain areas. This will not only help you refine your distinct value proposition but will also inform your marketing and product development initiatives.

Next, assess the competition landscape. **Who are your direct and indirect competitors? What are their distinct offerings, price structures, and marketing strategies?** Identify their strengths, limitations, and any unmet market needs that you may be able to capitalize on. This competitive intelligence will enable you to differentiate your company, create a distinct value offer, and establish a convincing advantage in the eyes of your target clients. Beyond understanding your customers and competition, it's critical to consider industry trends and market dynamics. What new technology, consumer habits, and regulatory developments could affect your online business? Staying on top of these industry-level insights can allow you to anticipate changes, adapt your tactics, and position your business for long-term success.

To collect this richness of market intelligence, use a range of research methodologies, including:

1. Conducting surveys and interviews with your target audience.

2. Examine industry data, market research, and rival websites.

3. Monitor social media and online forums.

4. Monitoring current trends and customer behaviour.

The findings from your extensive market research will serve as the cornerstone for your business plan, influencing everything from product creation and pricing to marketing tactics and expansion strategies. You'll be better able to make data-driven decisions and create a strong online business plan if you have a thorough awareness of your target market, the competitive environment, and industry dynamics.

Developing a Robust and Adaptive Business Strategy

Having established a firm grasp of your target market, creating a thorough yet flexible business plan is the next essential stage in launching your internet enterprise. From inspiration to execution, your business plan will act as a road map to keep you on track, flexible, and committed to your main objectives. Your online firm's unique value proposition is the keystone of your business plan; it is the unique advantage that you provide to clients. Make sure your UVP is compelling and differentiating for your target market by going over the findings from your market research again.

Create a clear and succinct mission statement that summarises your online business's purpose, values, and goals based on your unique selling point. This mission statement will be your guiding concept for all strategic and operational choices. Next, describe your business goals and the key performance indicators (KPIs) you'll use to track your progress. These objectives should be specific, measurable, attainable, relevant, and time-bound

(SMART), giving you a clear path to achievement.

After you've set your mission and objectives, dig into the specifics of your company strategy. How will you make money with your web business? What items or services will you be offering, and at what prices? Outline your pricing plan, distribution networks, and major partnership opportunities in order to build a viable and scalable firm. Consider essential areas such as product or service development, logistics and fulfilment, technological infrastructure, and team structure when creating your operational plan. Determine the resources, capabilities, and processes necessary to successfully launch an internet firm.

Notably, your business plan should include a complete financial estimate that details your launch costs, ongoing operating expenses, and revenue expectations. This financial analysis will not only assist you in obtaining finance, but will also inform your strategic decisions and assure the long-term profitability of your online enterprise. Finally, include a section on risk management and contingency plans. Anticipate potential obstacles, blockages, and external variables that may affect your firm, and devise methods to reduce these risks and react to changing market conditions.

CHAPTER 3

Building Your Online Presence - Website, Branding, and Digital Marketing.

Designing an Impactful and User-Friendly Website

Your website is like the physical storefront for your online business in this day and age. It is very important to how your customers see you, trust you, and interact with your business. A well-designed website that is easy for people to use not only shows off your goods or services, but it also shows what your brand stands for and who you are.

First, think about the user experience (UX) when you're building your online profile. Make sure your customers can easily find and buy the things they want by prioritizing easy browsing, clear product categorization, and a smooth checkout process. Use flexible design to make sure that your website works well on both desktop computers and mobile phones, so that it can adapt to the different ways that your target audience likes to browse.

Add high-quality, eye-catching images and video to your site to make your goods come to life and keep people interested. Make sure that the design of your website matches the visual character of your brand by using constant colors, fonts, and design elements that support the personality of your brand.

In addition to looking good, your website needs to have material that is both useful and interesting. Write interesting product descriptions, informative blog posts, and other useful content that solves the problems your customers are having and makes your brand look like an expert in its field.

Another important thing to think about when building your website is search engine optimization (SEO). Do a lot of study on keywords to find out what words and sentences people in your target audience are using to look for goods or services like yours. You can make your website more visible and higher up in search engine results by improving its content, information, and technical infrastructure. This will bring free traffic to your online business.

In the end, your website should be an extension of your brand that looks great, is easy to use, and gives users useful information that makes them want to interact, buy, and stay a customer.

Setting up a Strong Brand Identity

Building real links with your target audience, setting your products apart, and making a lasting impact in the crowded online marketplace all start with your brand name. A strong and consistent brand identity not only affects how people see your business, but it also helps you make choices about marketing and running the business.

Start by making a list of your brand's personality traits, key values, and the unique experience you want your customers to have. Your visual character, such as your image, color palette, font, and general style, will be built around these basic elements.

Hire a skilled graphic designer to help you make a unique and memorable visual business name. Your brand's style should come through in your image, and it should be easy to recognize across all of your digital and physical connections. Set a color scheme and fonts that will work the same on all of your marketing tools, including your website, social media pages, product packages, and more.

Besides the visuals, it's also important to find your brand's style and send messages that connect with your audience. Write a business story that shows what your company stands for, what you stand for, and how you can help your customers. Make sure that this brand voice shows up regularly in the text on your website, in product details, on social media, and in emails you send to customers.

As you build your online footprint, make sure that your brand personality is consistent across all of your digital connections. Use images, messages, and tone that are all in line with your brand to give your customers a seamless and memorable experience that sets your online business apart from the rest.

Using Digital Marketing Strategies That Work

In this digital age, you need a well-executed online marketing plan to get people to visit, interact with, and buy from your e-commerce business. You can reach your target audience, raise knowledge of your brand, and turn guests into loyal customers by using a variety of digital marketing strategies.

Start by building a strong social media profile on the sites where the people you want to reach are most likely to be. Create a content plan that fits with your brand and speaks to your fans. This should include a mix of showing off your products, teaching others, and fun interactions. Use Instagram Stories, product tags, and shoppable posts, among other social media tools, to get more people to your site and make sales.

Search engine optimization, or SEO, is another important tool for your digital marketing kit. Do a lot of study on keywords to find out what words and phrases your ideal customers use to look for goods or services just like yours. Improve your website's content, product details, and information to show up higher in search engine results and get more free traffic to your online store.

Content marketing is a great way to get people to know about your brand, show that you are an expert in your field, and bring more people to your website. Create a content plan that includes helpful blog posts, teaching videos, and other useful materials that solve the problems your customers are having and establish your brand as an expert in your field.

Email marketing is another very effective form of digital marketing that lets you build direct relationships with your customers and keep them interested as they make purchases. Make interesting email campaigns that show off your goods, send personalized deals, and keep your followers thinking about your brand.

You could also use paid advertising methods like search engine marketing (SEM), social media advertising, and display advertising to reach more people, target specific groups of customers, and get results that can be measured.

CHAPTER 4:

E-Commerce Essentials - Products, Payments, and Logistics

Optimizing Your Product Offering and Inventory Management

A carefully chosen and well-optimized product line is the heart of any successful online store. The products you choose, how much you charge for them, and how you handle your goods are all very important parts of running an online business.

Use the information you got from your market research to start by figuring out which goods or services your target audience wants and is willing to pay for. To make sure your product line fits the needs and wants of your ideal customers, look at what your customers want, what bothers them, and how they buy things.

Next, work on making the product better. Write product summaries that are interesting, SEO-friendly, and that stress the unique benefits and features of each item. Add to this high-quality, visually appealing product images and video material to make your products come to life and keep your buyers' attention.

Think carefully about your price plan, taking into account things like how much it costs to make the product, how much people want it, and how much other companies charge. Finding the best mix between making money and staying competitive is important for getting new customers and keeping the ones you already have.

Another important skill for e-commerce is being able to handle supplies well. Set up strong inventory tracking systems to keep an eye on stock levels, guess what customers will want, and make sure that popular items are restocked on time. This will not only improve the customer experience by reducing stock-outs, but it will also help you save money and run your business more efficiently.

Use data-driven insights to find products that aren't selling well or are moving slowly, and then use that information to decide whether to discontinue, lower, or expand those goods. To keep your online store well-organized and working well, you should always look at your product mix and make smart changes.

By improving how you list your products, set prices, and handle your inventory, you can give your customers a smooth and enjoyable shopping experience while also making your e-commerce business more profitable and effective.

Putting together solutions for seamless payment processing

A key part of any successful e-commerce business is handling payments quickly and safely. It is important to give your customers a smooth, safe, and secure payment process if you want to increase sales and build brand confidence over time.

First, look at which payment platforms and merchant service providers meet the needs of your online business and the people you want to buy from you. When choosing a payment method, think about things like transaction fees, handling speeds, scam protection, and the ability to accept payments from people all over the world.

Make sure your website's checkout process works with the payment handling platform you choose. This will make the customer journey easy and smooth. Give your customers a variety of ways to pay, such as credit/debit cards, digital wallets, and other choices, so you can accept the payment method that works best for them.

To build trust and keep your customers' private financial information safe, put payment security and scam prevention at the top of your list of priorities. To keep your purchases safe and your customers trusting you, use strong security measures like SSL encryption, PCI-DSS compliance, and advanced scam detection methods.

Keep up with how payments are changing, and be ready to change how you handle payments when new tools and industry trends come out. To keep up with your customers' changing wants and needs, you may need to add support for new payment methods like cryptocurrency or "buy now, pay later" choices.

By adding a reliable, safe, and flexible payment handling service without any problems, you can make the checkout process smooth for your customers, cut down on cart abandonment, and eventually get your e-commerce business more sales.

Streamlining operations for logistics and fulfillment

Order delivery and services that work well and are reliable are essential for an e-commerce business to be successful. Each link in the transportation chain, from storing goods and handling orders to shipping and delivery, can have a big effect on how happy your customers are, how much it costs to run your business, and your bottom line.

First, look at your order delivery choices. This includes things like shipping, packing, and storing your goods. Think about the pros and cons of hiring a third-party logistics (3PL) service versus doing these chores yourself. Control, scaling, and cost-effectiveness should all be taken into account.

If you're doing your own delivery, you should buy a good inventory management system to keep track of your stock, handle sales, and communicate with your shipping partners. Set up effective packing and sending processes to make sure that orders are processed quickly and correctly.

On the other hand, working with a trustworthy 3PL provider can give you many advantages, such as access to a large delivery system, improved processes, and the chance to grow your online store more efficiently. Carefully check out possible 3PL partners by looking at their skills, dependability, and how well they fit with your brand and customer service standards.

No matter what method you use for processing, you should make shipping and delivery the best they can be so your customers have a smooth and satisfying experience after they buy something. Give your customers a choice of shipping options, such as fast delivery and free standard shipping, so you can meet their needs and tastes.

Keep up with the newest technologies and trends in your field that can help your logistics, like checking orders in real time, automating picking and packing, and using eco-friendly shipping methods. By always making your operations and delivery better, you can keep customers coming back, lower your costs, and set up your e-commerce business for long-term success.

CHAPTER 5:

Funding Your Online Business Venture

Exploring Financing Options: Self-Funding, Investors, and Loans

A key step in making your e-commerce business idea a reality is getting the money you need. You can get money for your business in a number of different ways, each with its own pros and cons that depend on the size and stage of the business.

Funding Yourself

The easiest and most common way to get money for an online business is to finance it yourself. This means using your own money, assets, or savings to pay for the business's start-up costs and ongoing running costs. If you fund your own business, you won't have to answer to outside investors or loans, so you can make more decisions about how to run it.

However, self-funding comes with personal financial risk because you're putting your own money into the business. It's important to take a close look at your finances, figure out how much you can give, and make sure you have enough personal resources to support yourself and your business during the early stages of growth.

Looking for Investors

If you need a bigger starting investment for your online business, you might be able to get money from investors. Angel investors, venture capitalists, or sharing sites are all examples of this. Each has its own rules and requirements for investing.

Getting money from investors can give you the money you need to grow your business, add new goods, and expand your activities. Investors can also help your business succeed by connecting you with people in the same line of work, giving you practical advice, and acting as an adviser. But when you take money from investors, you usually give up some power over your business choices and some of your property.

How to Get Loans

You could also look into loan choices, such as lines of credit, small business loans, or loans for new businesses. This kind of loan can be gotten from regular banks, online lenders, or programs backed by the government. Loan financing can give you the money you need for your business while still letting you own and run it completely.

When looking for a loan, it's important to think about the interest rates, the terms of return, and any security or personal promises that may be needed. You should carefully look at your expected cash flow and make sure you can afford to pay back the loan without putting your online business at risk in the long run.

How to Make a Strong Pitch and Get Funding

No matter what method of financing you choose, you must make a well-thought-out, thorough, and effective pitch in order to get the money your online business needs.

Start by doing a lot of study on the specific needs, investment factors, and decision-making processes of the people you want to get money from, whether they are bankers, individual investors, or venture funders. You can then make your pitch fit their tastes, which will improve your chances of success.

The following important things should be in your pitch:

1. Executive Summary: Give a short summary of your online business, including what makes it special, who you're trying to reach, and how you plan to grow.

2. Market Analysis: Based on your in-depth market study, show that you have a deep understanding of the competition, industry trends, and customer requirements.

3. The business plan and the finances: Give a thorough breakdown of your online business's sources of income, costs, and financial forecasts, focusing on how it can grow and make money.

4. Team and Skills: Describe your original team and other important employees, focusing on their experience, skills, and history of success.

5. Funding Request and Use of Funds: Make it clear how much money you need and how you plan to use it to help your online business grow.

6. Exit Strategy: Write down your long-term goals and possible ways to get out of the business. This will help investors or loans understand how much money they might make.

Along with your pitch, you should have a well-thought-out, properly presented business plan that goes into more information about your online business. Potential investors or lenders will find this paper very helpful as they look at your e-commerce business to see if it will work and what its potential is.

During the funding process, you should be ready to answer questions, address concerns, and show that you can change and solve problems. Being sure of yourself, experienced, and quick to respond can help you build trust and get the money you need to start your dream online business.

CHAPTER 6:

Scaling Your Online Empire - Growth Strategies and Success Principles

Leveraging Data Analytics to Drive Informed Decision-Making

As your e-commerce business grows and changes, making decisions based on data becomes more and more important to take your online company to new heights. By using data analytics, you can learn a lot about how your customers behave, how well your marketing works, and how efficiently your operations run. This will help you make smart decisions that will lead to long-term growth.

Set up strong data tracking and reporting tools to get a full picture of how your online business is doing. Use online analytics tools, like Google Analytics, to keep an eye on important numbers like website traffic, sales data, conversion rates, and where customers come from to buy. You can quickly find trends, patterns, and places to improve by combining data from your e-commerce platform, marketing platforms, and other business systems into a single display.

Learn as much as you can about your target group by digging deep into customer info. To make specific customer profiles and characters, look at demographics, psychographics, and viewing and buying habits. This detailed information about your customers will help you make better products, set prices, and run more effective marketing efforts that reach the right people. This will help you better meet the changing wants and needs of your online customers.

Keep a close eye on how your marketing is doing and keep track of the return on investment (ROI) for all of your digital outlets, programs, and strategies. To get the most out of your marketing efforts, you should always be testing and improving your tactics. This includes finding the best ways to spend money on ads, distribute content, and get customers involved.

Use data analytics to improve the working performance of your e-commerce business as well. Look at measures like product turnover, order handling times, shipping and transportation performance, and customer service to find ways to make your business run more smoothly and find ways to improve customer service.

By teaching your employees to think like data scientists and giving your team the tools to use analytics results, you can make smart decisions that will help your online business grow and make money over time.

Using growth strategies that can be scaled up and adding new sources of income

As your online store grows, it's important to use scalable growth strategies and add new ways to make money to make sure it stays successful and strong over time.

Look for ways to grow your business in new areas. The internet can help you reach customers all over the world, so don't limit yourself to local or regional markets. Think about things like language, currency, and culture tastes when making changes to your website and marketing for people from other countries.

Add to your product line by adding linked or complementary items that meet the changing wants of your customers. Look at sales data, customer reviews, and market trends to find chances to add new products, make existing ones bigger, or even make your own brands.

Take advantage of the benefits of smart relationships and agreements to reach new groups of customers, find new ways to sell your products or services, and get access to new marketing outlets. Look for ways to work together with partner marketers, celebrities, or brands that are similar to yours to reach more people through cross-promotion.

Add subscription-based models, ongoing revenue streams, or value-added services to your business to make your income sources more diverse. This can mean giving your customers ongoing value through membership programs, product packages, or special content and tools.

Always look at your pricing tactics and make changes to them as needed. Try different price points, deals, and discounts until you find the best balance between making money and appealing to customers. Use lessons from data to find chances for dynamic pricing, volume-based deals, or customizable offers that will help you make the most money and stay ahead of the competition.

As you grow your online business, make sure that your operational infrastructure, transportation, and customer service systems can handle the extra work and demand. Invest in technology solutions that can be expanded, make your supply chain work better, and put together a team of skilled, flexible workers who can help your business grow.

By using these flexible growth strategies and getting money from different sources, you'll be able to handle changes in the market, take advantage of new possibilities, and set up your e-commerce business for long-term, steady growth.

Creating a culture of new ideas and constant improvement

In the ever-changing and fast-paced world of e-commerce, you need a mindset of innovation and constant improvement to stay ahead of the competition and make sure your online business continues to succeed.

Encourage your employees to think like entrepreneurs, which will allow them to be creative, question the status quo, and look for new ideas and solutions. Encourage people to talk to each other openly, work together to solve problems, and be open to trying new things and learning from their wins and mistakes.

Review your business plans, working methods, and the

experience of your customers on a regular basis to find ways to make them better. Get feedback from your customers, workers, and experts in the field to learn useful things that can help you come up with new ideas.

Put in place an organized way to test and confirm new ideas, like pilot programs, A/B testing, or customer polls. This lets you get insights from data, lower your risks, and make smart choices about whether your ideas can work and be scaled up.

Develop a mindset of flexibility and speed so that your business can react quickly to changes in the market, new technologies, and customers' changing tastes. Keep an eye on customer behavior, industry trends, and what your competitors are doing, and be ready to change your strategies and methods as needed.

Give your team members the freedom to own their work, encourage them to share their thoughts, and praise and reward creative problem-solving and thinking outside the box. This can help your company develop a competitive energy and drive, which will help your e-commerce business grow and be successful.

Also, think about spending money on your team's professional growth and ongoing learning. To help your workers stay up to date on the latest e-commerce trends, technologies, and best practices, encourage them to attend industry conferences, take online courses, and join training programs.

By making innovation and constant improvement a part of your online business, you'll be able to predict and respond to changing market conditions, stay ahead of the competition, and always give your customers the best value. These are the qualities of a successful e-commerce empire.

Here are a few examples of successful e-commerce businesses that have implemented innovative growth strategies:

1. Wayfair - Leveraging Data and Personalization
Wayfair, the online home goods retailer, has achieved remarkable growth by harnessing the power of data analytics and personalization. The company collects extensive customer data, including browsing behavior, product preferences, and purchase history, to create highly customized shopping experiences. Wayfair's algorithms analyze this data to make personalized product recommendations, target marketing campaigns, and optimize pricing - all of which have contributed to its impressive sales and customer loyalty.

2. Glossier - Building a Cult-Like Brand Community.
Glossier, the direct-to-consumer beauty brand, has succeeded in building a highly engaged and loyal customer base through its innovative approach to branding and community-building. The company leverages social media, user-generated content, and a focus on digital experiences to foster a sense of belonging and exclusivity among its customers. By creating a strong brand identity and cultivating a devoted community, Glossier has been able to drive sustainable growth and expand its product offerings over time.

3. Amazon - Diversifying Revenue Streams Amazon, the e-commerce giant, has successfully diversified its revenue streams beyond its core online retail business. The company has expanded into cloud computing (AWS), digital advertising, and even healthcare, leveraging its vast customer base, technological capabilities, and logistical infrastructure to capitalize on new growth opportunities. By continuously exploring new avenues for revenue generation, Amazon has solidified its position as a dominant player in the e-commerce landscape.

4. Zappos - Prioritizing Customer Experience Zappos, the online shoe and clothing retailer, has built its success on prioritizing an exceptional customer experience. The company is known for its responsive customer service, flexible return policies, and personalized interactions with customers. By placing a strong emphasis on customer satisfaction, Zappos has been able to cultivate brand loyalty and drive repeat business, even in a highly competitive industry.

5. Shopify - Empowering Entrepreneurship Shopify, the e-commerce platform, has achieved remarkable growth by empowering entrepreneurs and small businesses to establish their online presence. The company's user-friendly platform, comprehensive suite of tools, and extensive partner ecosystem have made it easier for aspiring e-commerce entrepreneurs to launch and scale their businesses. Shopify's focus on democratizing e-commerce has allowed it to tap into a vast and growing market of online merchants.

CHAPTER 7:

Sustaining Long-Term Success - Operations, Finances, and Legal Considerations

Optimizing Business Operations and Assembling the Right Team.

To succeed in the online market and make money in the long run, you need to streamline your business processes and put together a skilled team that works well together.

Start by looking at your current business processes, figuring out what could be done better, and then putting in place systems and methods that will make them more productive and scalable. Use software for managing supplies, systems for handling orders, and tools for customer relationship management (CRM) to simplify and improve important business tasks.

As your e-commerce business grows, you should carefully look at your organizational system and the people you need to hire. Put together a broad, cross-functional team with the skills and knowledge to help you reach your growth goals. Some jobs that fall into this category are digital marketers, web developers, data scientists, customer service reps, and transportation managers.

Give your team members the tools, training, and freedom they need to do well in their jobs by giving them empowerment. Encourage imagination, innovation, and a shared commitment to the company's success by creating an atmosphere that is open, honest, and purpose-driven.

Make sure everyone in your company is accountable and on the same page by setting up clear ways to communicate, make decisions, and handle performance. Regular check-ins, feedback sessions, and performance reviews can help you find and fix any problems or places where your operations could be better.

As your online business grows, you might want to think about the pros and cons of hiring or outsourcing certain tasks, like delivery, customer service, or managing your IT infrastructure. This can help you focus on what you do best while using outside knowledge and tools to make your operations run more smoothly.

By making your business operations run more smoothly and building a strong, cooperative team, you'll be able to handle the constantly changing e-commerce scene, adapt quickly to changes in the market, and keep your online business growing and making money in the long term.

Taking care of taxes, finances, and staying profitable

For your e-commerce business to be successful in the long run, you need to be able to handle your money well. For strategic planning and making smart decisions, you need to have a full picture of your company's financial health. This includes keeping accurate financial records, maximizing cash flow, handling taxes, and making sure the business stays profitable.

Set up a solid accounting system to keep accurate records of your business's financial progress. This could mean putting in place enterprise resource planning (ERP) tools, hiring a professional financial service, or putting together a finance team to work in-house. You should look over your income statements, balance sheets, and cash flow statements on a regular basis to find patterns and find any problems. This will help you make smart choices about investments, product management, and price.

Carefully handle your working capital to make sure you have enough cash on hand and to lower the risk of problems with your cash flow. Keep an eye on your accounts due and receivable, make sure you have the right amount of goods, and look into financing options like lines of credit or inventory financing to keep your cash flow healthy and meet your business needs.

For your e-commerce business, make sure you follow all tax rules and filing requirements. Keep up with the latest changes to tax laws, sales tax connection rules, and income tax obligations. To make sure you file your taxes on time and correctly, work closely with a skilled lawyer or tax professional.

To stay profitable, you should always look at your price tactics and cost models. Look at your gross and net profit margins to find ways to cut costs and use that information to help you decide on prices, sales, and discounts that will help your bottom line.

As your e-commerce business grows, you might want to add advanced data analytics, predicting models, and strategic financial planning to your financial management skills. This can help you predict and react to changes in the market, find new ways to make money, and better use your resources to make your business more profitable in the long run.

By putting good money management first, you can keep your e-commerce business healthy, long-lasting, and profitable. This will set your company up for continued success in the ever-changing online market.

Getting around the laws and rules that affect online businesses

The rules and laws that govern e-commerce can be hard to understand and are always changing. You need to pay close attention and follow them exactly to make sure your online business stays legal and successful in the long run. Thinking about these things carefully and ahead of time can help you avoid problems, look out for your business's best interests, and build a strong base for long-term growth.

Before you do anything else, make sure that your online store is fully licensed and listed according to the laws and rules in your area. This could mean getting the business licenses, sales tax permits, and any badges or permits relevant to your field that you need to run your business.

Get to know all the customer protection laws, data privacy rules, and laws that apply to online shopping, like the CAN-SPAM Act, the General Data Protection Regulation (GDPR), and the Payment Card Industry Data Security Standard (PCI DSS). Protect your customers' personal and financial information by putting in place policies, procedures, and technical defenses. Make sure your marketing is clear and legal, and keep your online deals safe.

Review and write your website's privacy policy, terms of service, and return and refund policy with care to make sure they clearly explain your company's rules and protect your legal interests. Talk to an experienced lawyer to make sure these papers are complete, sound from a legal point of view, and follow the rules and laws in the places you want to sell to.

As your e-commerce business grows, keep international trade rules, customs fees, and the needs of cross-border transactions in mind. Get to know the rules that apply, and if you need help navigating the complicated world of global e-commerce, think about teaming up with shipping providers or law experts.

Additionally, keep up with any improvements or changes in the laws and rules that could affect your e-commerce business, and be ready to change your policies and practices to match. This could mean keeping an eye on changes in areas like privacy, buyer rights, product safety, and intellectual property rules.

EPILOGUE

As you shut the last pages of "The 7-Step Formula for Launching a Six-Figure Online Business," realize that your entrepreneurial adventure has only just started. Armed with the information and tactics presented in these pages, you have the keys to open the doors of opportunity in the digital world. Accept the difficulties, cherish the successes, and make this book the foundation of your continuous success narrative. Your future as a successful internet company owner awaits go out and conquer!

AFTERWORD

In finishing "The 7-Step Formula for Launching a Six-Figure Online Business," I'd want to convey my deepest appreciation for joining me on this transforming journey. As you negotiate the fast-paced world of business, keep in mind that success is a never-ending journey. Continue to refine your plans, embrace innovation, and nurture your entrepreneurial spirit.

Your goal of building a six-figure internet company is about more than simply making money; it's about living a life of freedom, satisfaction, and influence. Each step you take demonstrates your dedication and perseverance. Accept the obstacles, learn from failures, and appreciate each accomplishment along the road.

Remember to be adaptable and creative as you use the ideas discussed in this book. The digital world is always evolving, providing limitless opportunity for those eager to innovate and remain ahead of the curve.

Above all, be confident in yourself and your goals. You have the ability to build the life and business that you want. Trust the process, keep focused on your objectives, and never underestimate the power of your ambitions.

Thank you again for letting me be a part of your business path. May this book serve as a guiding light as you follow your goals and establish the six-figure internet company of your dreams. I wish you riches, success, and satisfaction in all your undertakings.

ABOUT THE AUTHOR

Jonas Charles Kpabitey

Born in the bustling city of Accra, Ghana, Jonas Charles Kpabitey discovered his passion for storytelling at a young age. Raised in a family that valued education and literature, Jonas immersed himself in books from an early age, fostering a deep appreciation for the power of words.

Jonas's journey as a writer began during his formative years at the University of Ghana, where he pursued a degree in English Literature. Inspired by the rich cultural tapestry of his homeland and the diverse experiences of his peers, Jonas found his voice as a storyteller, weaving tales that reflected the complexities of life in Ghana and beyond.

During his time at university, Jonas distinguished himself not only as a diligent student but also as a prolific writer. His keen observations of human nature and his ability to capture the nuances of everyday life soon caught the attention of readers and fellow writers alike.

Jonas delves into themes of identity, belonging, and the search for meaning in a rapidly changing world. Drawing on his own experiences and those of his peers, he crafts a narrative that resonates with readers of all backgrounds, inviting them to explore the universal truths that bind us together as human beings.

Beyond his literary pursuits, Jonas remains deeply committed to using his platform as a writer. Whether through his fiction or his activism, he continues to inspire others to embrace their own stories and to strive for a more inclusive and compassionate world.

As Jonas Charles Kpabitey continues to hone his craft and share his unique perspective with the world, his voice promises to be a beacon of hope and inspiration for generations to come.

www.ingramcontent.com/pod-product-compliance
Lightning Source LLC
Chambersburg PA
CBHW050245230526
45470CB00005B/2125